Soul Circuit

NAVIGATING THE MYSTERIES OF INNER CONNECTION

Shivali Kalra

BLUEROSE PUBLISHERS
India | U.K.

Copyright © Shivali Kalra 2024

All rights reserved by author. No part of this publication may be reproduced, stored in a retrieval system or transmitted in any form or by any means, electronic, mechanical, photocopying, recording or otherwise, without the prior permission of the author. Although every precaution has been taken to verify the accuracy of the information contained herein, the publisher assume no responsibility for any errors or omissions. No liability is assumed for damages that may result from the use of information contained within.

BlueRose Publishers takes no responsibility for any damages, losses, or liabilities that may arise from the use or misuse of the information, products, or services provided in this publication.

For permissions requests or inquiries regarding this publication, please contact:

BLUEROSE PUBLISHERS
www.BlueRoseONE.com
info@bluerosepublishers.com
+91 8882 898 898
+4407342408967

ISBN: 978-93-6261-012-6

Cover design: Tahira
Typesetting: Tanya Raj Upadhyay

First Edition: September 2024

PREFACE

Addressing love, compassion, mystery, mysticism and life. The seekers shall find their sentence, their story in the very words. This collection of poems will strike those who carry within them a spark of truth, desire and curiosity. May these words become your shining light and connect to your soul. May this book provide you a window to the human experience offering insights into love, loss, joy, wonder, sorrow and everything in between as the story unfolds. I am here pushing the boundaries of what poetry can be and do, making it more vibrant and exciting. Welcome to my world of narrative poetry.

Poetry is eternal and a poet's soul is immortal'

©□SoulCircuit

ACKNOWLEDGEMENT

Thanking each and everyone with whom my path ever crossed as they became a part of my life's enriched experiences. Thanking my kids Sanah and Amaan for being my constant support and for adding endless joy in my life. Thanking all my close friends, family, cousins, mentors and soul sisters who inspired me and encouraged me to live and to write stories that matter.

©□SoulCircuit

BOOK DESCRIPTION

Are you someone who is interested in finding your own meaning in metaphorical components of structure and vocabulary provided by the poet in the form of a story ? If Yes, then dive into the expansion of story written in verse that shall open the doors for you to explore word choice and literary devices in a way that only poetry can provide. It's a rare book of narrative poetry. The flow of poems and the theme centres around a transformative journey of a woman named Mira. Each and every line of these poems takes you to the depth of different emotions, moods and expressions that she has experienced at some point in her life. Though author's narrative revolves around a woman being a central character, still it is a good read for all, irrespective of gender. This book explains how we humans are connected to poetry, which is reflected through parts and phases of our lives. If you don't mind flowing with widely accepted theory of basic emotions and their expressions such as calmness, sadness, happiness, joy, fear, anger, surprise and disgust then this book is for you. These strong feelings are derived from one's mood, circumstances or relationships with others. Though in these modern times we may remain oblivious to the pervasive power of poetry, to trigger, heal and transform our mind, yet each poem would relate to a certain period in your life. All the poems are very well crafted and unfiltered, touching the essence of ups and downs, highs and lows of life. The simple rhyming words of these lyrical poems in addition with the use of monostich and couplets in the cluster, make it more interesting to read. These poems string together the inspirational story of a character named 'Mira' in a very subtle way. Through this reading experience you'll see what poems do. They take you deep into the sea of emotions bringing different stories to life. When the words are in harmony with your thoughts that you strongly identify and resonate with, you'll feel as if, you are the central character and it's your story. In clear and simple words author has set each work in its social, cultural, and literary context. Do you know that poetry has its therapeutic quality? It definitely heals, and fosters introspection, encourages authenticity, and aids in articulating the nuances of one's ever evolving identity.

Like the author says 'You come out of it alive, when words bleed of a torn soul'

©□SoulCircuit

DEDICATION

This first book of mine as an Author is dedicated to my son and my daughter who are the light of my life and who fill my heart with joy.

Dedicated to family, friends and my soul sisters and all those people who have survived the impossible and people who change the lives of others by living as an example and sharing their knowledge.

TABLE OF CONTENTS

CHAPTER 1 POET'S SOUL 1

CHAPTER 2 WANNA BE ME 5

CHAPTER 3 WINGS OF TRANSFORMATION 11

CHAPTER 4 LAYERS 15

CHAPTER 5 GREYS - NOW AND FOREVER 19

CHAPTER 6 CHAOTIC PARADISE 23

CHAPTER 7 LONE TYPIST 27

CHAPTER 8 DREAMER'S DIARIES 29

CHAPTER 9 BEAUTIFUL TALES 33

CHAPTER 10 IMAGINARY BALLET 37

CHAPTER 11 TAMED GUITAR 39

CHAPTER 12 LOVE BEAT 41

CHAPTER 13 ENDLESS LOVE 45

CHAPTER 14 ONLY WHISPERS 49

CHAPTER 15 RHYTHM AND RHYME 53

CHAPTER 16 ROMANCE 55

CHAPTER 17 QUEEN 57

CHAPTER 18 AGONY	61
CHAPTER 19 MYSTERIES LIVE AND MYSTERIOUS ARE KNOWN	65
CHAPTER 20 DESIRE	69
CHAPTER 21 MYSTIC WALK	73
ABOUT THE AUTHOR	77

CHAPTER 1
POET'S SOUL

Everyone is a poet, in poetry one is free

We are all poets and each one of us is a poet. In poetry we are free. There are moments in our life when we are so inspired with our feelings of love that it gives us a way to string words. When something about the universe awakens our soul and then words become a channel for our feelings to pour. There is power in words and pen becomes our sword.

While growing up, each one of us has had a romantic notion of getting into the character of a poet, spurting out poems effortlessly in praise or in pain. With a bottle in one hand and lover in the other. When you want to voice and to be heard you become a poet. But the truth is we have only few poets as brooding geniuses, just because they are the ones who have a true gift of invoking extreme tremendous emotions in us, let it be sadness or excitement. Poets create their own language, they find a way to conjure strong emotions from words and that's what many people are looking for. Some relatable, interestingly intense emotion.

Poetry is many things, it may never or always rhyme. It's ease and fluidity are both reliant on the splendour that created it.

So let's dive into the poetic narrative of Mira's life and her story of scars to stars.

IT'S A POET'S SOUL
IT'S A POET'S SOUL
When you find music in the nature,
Everywhere sound, your ears can capture :
Singing with the tunes of the falling waters
Finding Rythm in the flocking feathers ;
Noisy streams, sounds of birds, call of the animals and the cloud that roars…
Dancing along the essence of music while it pours !!
IT'S A POET'S SOUL
IT'S A POET'S SOUL
When you can listen to the silent words,
Your quest for truth behind reality is told ;
The sadness, shadowed by the unreal happiness,
Nothing actually feeds your eagerness…
IT'S A POET'S SOUL
IT'S A POET'S SOUL
Where dreaming is reality
And love is so deep,
that all emotions floor behind the closed doors ;
Your soul is still lonely
While surrounded by millions in this world,
Saying it all in a piece of paper
While all this can easily be told ;
The universe keeps guessing for you,
Whereas
This is where your story unfolds….
IT'S A POET'S SOUL
IT'S A POET'S SOUL

**CHAPTER 2
WANNA BE ME**

Tired of being you , wanna be in the world free of blues

It was one unusual autumn rainy night. Like autumn weather changes all the time so does Mira's life. In this dark rainy night Mira was screaming to death. The sound of the rain and the thundering was enough to silence her voice. Struggling and screaming, she laid on the bed bleeding furiously from her mouth with a broken tooth, a disarranged jaw, blue swollen eyes and red, majorly swollen nose. Not only this, it also seemed like she escaped an attempt of getting stabbed by scissors in her stomach. Yes! It was a narrow escape with definitely a cut on her stomach.

In the middle of all this chaos there was this continuous bang on the door. Mira's daughter Minaj and Mira's Cousin Priya who came rushing from the next room after hearing the painful screams were kicking the door with all their might, trying to break it open.

But here he was, not stopping at all. More so, to stop her from screaming, he sat right on top of her chest trying to suffocate her. It was this huge man trying to smother her with a pillow. Who was this man ? he was none other than Mira's husband Rav. Rav had gone crazy and mad like every other day, he just wanted to kill her in the fit of madness and started pushing the pillow hard on her while putting all his weight and pressing her on chest.

'Papa please open the door 'little Minaj shouted while her aunt was banging the door. This time it was a mightier kick which helped the door break open. They saw Mira who was lying unconscious on the bed struggling for her life. Minaj this little girl on the other hand was so confused and terrified, witnessing something like a crime scene, she didn't know what to doshould she try to save her mom or should she pacify and distract her little brother Anvit who came rushing to the room. She took him back to the other room and asked him to sleep so that he doesn't see, listen or grasp the situation. In the meantime Priya was trying to bring Mira back to her consciousness and gave her the first aid. Fortunately Mira came back to life. But she was not in a state to talk or to move. She became unconscious again.

This story is not of one Mira and her kids but hundreds and thousands of Mira's whose inner self along with the physical gets hurt, violated, squelched and diminished. These stories seem unreal, living in this modern age and era. But they are real, these Mira's are still living among us. Those who have lost their sense of self and identity, because with all these years of faking and pretending happiness, they become masters of masking the hell they are living in. They have created a double life and have learnt to conceal the pain with a brave face as if everything is perfectly fine. This could be your story or anybody's story, because Domestic Violence does not discriminate. It is gender neutral and anyone can fall prey to it. The only difference is some escape and some lose their life.

I just wanna be me
Coz I'm tired of being you
Wanna be in the world free of blues;
In this journey where I have been walking with you, I want you to be with me.
I see isolation when I dare to take few steps my way,
I smile when I feel like crying
Words don't come easy as I want to speak;
I have the fear of falling apart but I still wanna hold on ;
Am I losing hope ?
Give me some clue,
Lead me towards sunshine and
Let me be me
Let me be me !
Rinsing my worries in the pool of wines,
Getting naughty as the moon shines;
Let me be me
Let me be me !
Love the way it's happening
Seeking and finding all the barriers within me,
Let me be me
Let me be me !
You hold no promises
I can't discover your mysteries,
I'm giving you up
I'm breaking free;
Let me be me
Let me be me……

CHAPTER 3
WINGS OF TRANSFORMATION

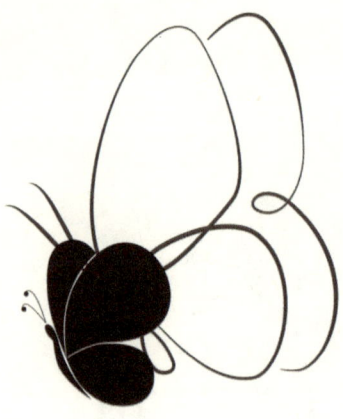

Change is scary, but only through fear you will undergo a beautiful transformation

The escape was not easy. Her fear had vanished, disappeared and her journey of self discovery and redefining the warrior within had started. For way more than a decade Mira endured extreme emotional, mental and physical pain. Not only that she even suffered financial abuse at the hands of her husband. She was isolated, broken and defeated to the length that everything from where she went, whom she spoke to, her words, her time and her finances were controlled. She had given up on her dreams and aspirations. It wasn't only her life that was in jeopardy but also that of her children. Mira who was always afraid to to tell anyone about what was happening with her, at her so called home, gained some courage after her survival. Along with that came the awareness and enlightenment that the trauma she was facing on a daily basis was not normal. She started thinking straight, whether it is better to leave and to live or to succumb to the consequences.

The violence that she had endured was just a beginning of her story. Suddenly something shifted and her wings of transformation grew. Instead of mourning the pain, exhaustion and agony she was ready to face the world and fly on and on and on.

> Time stood still in her vagueness
> Where the darkness descended;
> Suddenly a stroke of life moved in her,
> She gathered all her broken pieces
> Removing the shard that was piercing hard through her soul;
> Soon before she knew,
> Her wings of transformation were born and
> She became a dragonfly who was already on her way……

CHAPTER 4
LAYERS

Find music in your soul

It was one special morning, among the soft breeze and the silence, the chirping and melodious singing of the birds was clearly heard. In this lush green garden, Mira was sitting on her swing sipping tea from her cup while listening to her favourite music. This was everyday routine for Mira, she found her peace and solace in nature. These 20 to 30 minutes every morning would work as an energy booster for her. That day something unusual happened and she had gone into a deep trance while listening to the music and in that very moment she had a mental change.

Something inside her shifted and she started transforming into a warrior as if the phoenix had born from the ashes. Her layers of fear were falling and fearlessness had started covering her.

> Under the layers of fearful emotions,
> She found a verse that could bare her soul.....

CHAPTER 5
GREYS - NOW AND FOREVER

You are always walking into the grey, there is no black and white
i say

The experience of life so far taught Mira that it's not about being right or wrong. It's just about the perception and everyone sees life through their own lens. It's not about true or false but circumstances and experiences. It's not about success and failure but mere luck. She understood that in life we cannot change the cards we are dealt, it's just how we play the hand. She realized it's not yes or no but subjective, it is never black and white but grey. Life is not about knowing all the answers but about being comfortable in its uncertainty. When she was enlightened with this knowledge, she had more compassion for herself and others. She realized that even she is allowed to make mistakes, to voice her voice and to have a narrative.

Its all about the hues of grey,
Pain, hurt and misery to which all are falling prey …..
Jiving to the tunes of miseries
Smiling in a jiffy and crying over a tiffy,
Here's a call to an endless storm that goes behind all the individual stories ;
There's no Black and White I say
It's all Grey which is here to stay….
Love, desires and attractions might take you a few shades lighter ;
While being a perpetrator, gives you a million shades darker….
Not even a single human can be a complete Frey :
As there are so many blends in the shades of Grey ;
There's no Black and White I say
It's all Grey which is here to stay….
Exploring this nuanced terrain,
Where you seldom find rest in heart and brain ;
Mysteries that are not easy to solve,
They are snuggling in comfort and are still to evolve….
There's no Black and White I say
It's all Grey which is here to stay….
Greys are here Now and Forever
To make your soul tremble in terror ;
Nothing explains right or wrong,
It says of your feelings of good and bad for long…
There's no Black and White I say
It's all Grey which is here to stay !!!
It's all Grey which is here to stay !!!

CHAPTER 6
CHAOTIC PARADISE

Even in the darkest dark, her light would shine

From bleakness she was moving into light, from self doubt to self growth. She made her pain the reason to rise and shine. As synchronicity beamed, she started heading towards light leaving behind the grey cloud which had spread far and wide. As she was moving towards light, she could see herself as a damsel so bright. In a royal silken white dress who was dancing her way through the night. Her light had become so bright that she was sparkling in glitter and stardust, lighting up and bringing the sparkle and shine to everyone she met and crossed path with.

> Beauty of a woman lies in the depth of her eyes;
> In the silence behind her cries
> In her smiles beyond the toughest miles,
> Where she still manages to shine;
> Lighting up everything and everyone,
> Lying in and among her chaotic paradise

CHAPTER 7
LONE TYPIST

Solitude is not loneliness, it's the journey of self

Mira had started spreading happiness, light and smiles wherever she went. Despite being a happy and chirpy soul, she would like to come back to her solace, her inner self every now and then to reflect within and conquer the universe inside becoming one with her core. That time wad hers alone and she deeply connected with the world inside that her centre hides. She learnt to become her own guru.

> She was a lone typist,
> Would type in pieces…..
> But whenever she did,
> She would leave pieces of her soul !!

CHAPTER 8
DREAMER'S DIARIES

To dream is to be

She was always a dreamer. A dreamer then when she was a baby and a dreamer when she celebrated her climb forthright into the beauty of her prime and a dreamer now even with the years passing sublime. All set to conquer life. There happened a paradigm shift and she is now more dedicated to dream big and give wings to her dreams to let them unfurl into reality and viewed this world in wonder, surprise and gratification.

Like Mira one should never stop dreaming !!

Sleeping with the visions of glory,
They have their own different world of backstory
Here come the dreamers ;
For them dreaming is the only reality
Where they are most comfortable in their manner of frivolity,
They have eyes to see things far and beyond
And can listen to the world which
does not respond,
Here come the dreamers ;
Their diaries keep the spectrum of emotional wavelength
But what they are to the world is :
Source Of Strength !!!
They can hide storms behind their smiles
And would walk the loners miles,
Here come the dreamers ;
They know of theories that say :-
The greater life's pain, The greater life replies
They find happiness in small little things
But have always furnished the world with greater glazings !!!
Pulled and Pushed by all they can see ;
Only as much as they can dream, they can be
Only as much as they can dream, they can be……

CHAPTER 9
BEAUTIFUL TALES

Her body is a journal which tells a story she has lived

This night was silent, lonely as if everything and everyone was resting. Mira was sleeping and suddenly a sharp and shrilly sound of the past woke her up. It was like as if something had stopped her heart. She lay still in bed with closed eyes thinking to deal with all the nightmares and the reflections of the past, promising herself a new story a new life.

Like Mira everyone has to struggle to find their confidence time and again. To forget the past and welcome the future.

She is both beautiful and wild,
Living in the Greek world as Ancient as Time.
For the body she has, she holds that in her pride ;
Curvy or full,
It's all about her shades of love
For the world that's cruel,
She still chooses to be a dove !!
For what she sees in the mirror is a reflection of beautiful tales ;
Few gone, some untold and a number of more to unfold…..

CHAPTER 10
IMAGINARY BALLET

Faith

Mira understood one thing about life as she had seen her own astonishing light. That, one must stop seeking control. As soon as you start owning your story, with it you start to roll.

This is not a poem, not a narrative but merely some words, to make you understand that the only way forward is to go with the flow. So don't stop yourself and just keep going.

> I'm a story inscribed in an imaginary ballet,
> A poem in continuous motion
> Lumbered, flawed yet flawless;
> Picking up steps and treasured learnings,
> All in his faith and glory…

CHAPTER 11
TAMED GUITAR

Her heart is free and untamed

Mira became completely fearless in her dramatic performance of life. She had become so passionate about life that if she would live as society wanted her to live, she would never be truly happy and fulfilled. For society does not want women to wander. In fact there were few people who wanted to see her fail in her dream of living a fulfilled life. But she was determined to break all barriers. Her idea of freedom was to have freedom of thought, freedom to follow her passion, her dreams and yet be close to her loved ones. In one way she was tamed and in the other untamed.

> Her untamed heart would play melodies on a tamed guitar
> ...

CHAPTER 12
LOVE BEAT

Dance is the hidden language of the soul

Until a few days ago, Mira had completely felt empty from inside. She had experienced people who were not loving or valuing her but completely eating her away. That's when she started feeling the pain of her insides and the loneliness again. Her realization of self that had happened lately changed her forever no matter how intense the past pain was. She got it all figured out now. She accepted her story and owned it in the thick of it, without seeking answers and without any pretty ribbon to tie it all up in. But in her moments of clarity, she did believe with every fibre of her being, that the worse is behind her and now she's heading towards the best. She started following her passion and started working hard towards it. She started falling in love but this time with her own self.

She twirls and spins to the rythm in the music,
She's pain she's fear
She's bliss and she's tear;
In a flash moment
With each of her movement,
She breaks all the walls to have her emotional release.
She's an artist who narrates through expression and ease;
Yes she's a dancer, her soul is entwined to the love beat !!!!

CHAPTER 13
ENDLESS LOVE

His eyes held an endless kind of love for her

As Mira was progressing in her work, completely focused on life, she bumped into someone. Dev, a handsome, cultured and a decent man Mira met by chance. When she saw him she felt as if she is seeing her own reflection, completely alike, so similar that it felt surreal. Dev and Mira chatted endlessly in their first meeting. It all felt so familiar. Same thoughts, ideologies, values, likes and dislikes. They had so much in common. Dev and Mira never expressed their emotions and how they felt for each other but some where in her heart she knew, if life would have brought them together in early years this would have been the best match for her. She believed at times one must leave things unsaid. She had become so scared of love to let anyone in her life that she pushed Dev away friend zoning him because she believed every story doesn't have to be a love story and love eventually hurts, so it's better to stay away.

> OH YA LOVE ! However small the word
> It's power holds the entire universe…
> When you bloom in love, you grow, prosper and glow
> When it drains you,
> Pain, misery and hurt serve well as a curse…
> Love is an endless try,
> As it tempts you to the mysterious world of being owned and loved by someone ;
> You enjoy and roll in utmost beauty and joy
> Until it makes you cry….
> Still you won't stop,
> For your soul longs for a soulmate
> To revere, to love, to take a beautiful journey together
> Through harsh and silent waves
> Ultimately reaching the final gate !!!
> The Story Continues……

CHAPTER 14
ONLY WHISPERS

He captured her essence into the mere words

No doubt Mira was scared of falling in love or letting anyone enter her life but somewhere inside her she wanted to experience this deep true love. In those lonely nights she used to think that she definitely deserves all the love, care and affection and the best partner ever who would understand not only her words but even her silence. In reality she had no strength to try again because any love worth having is a gamble. Either you win or you lose it all. She was too scared to take the risk. She wanted some sort of convincing, some assurance. But does it work this way? No it doesn't. Relationships naturally evolve with time and one has to take the risk.

Only whispers my heart will ever hear
are from the one, who shall turn me into a beautiful poetry
!!!

CHAPTER 15
RHYTHM AND RHYME

At the touch of his love she became a poetess

Mira was so grateful to God that she crossed her path with Dev. She believed that true divine love is not in ownership but in letting go. She was happy that at least at some point in life she met someone who felt so familiar and it was no less than a miracle.

> You fit in my poems so well, that my words become lyrics and my lyrics find rhythm and they rhyme

CHAPTER 16
ROMANCE

Love is their favourite feeling

As Mira was progressing on her journey towards self love, she started feeling and looking more beautiful. She would glow and sparkle as if millions and millions of stars shined on her and covered her. She also started seeing the world in beauty and wonder. She saw beauty as far as her eyes could see. This divine positive shift inside her always lead her to something more positive. She would find happiness in little things.

> She was so romantic about the mysterious moon because it would stay all night to find the sparkle in her eyes !!

CHAPTER 17
QUEEN

Her soul is royalty, she turns pain into power

Accessing the sovereignty within, Mira had become the best version of herself. She started feeling and behaving like a queen, someone who had fully found herself and embraced it. A woman who always spoke to herself and others with utmost kindness and love had shed all her self-limiting beliefs. She had also become completely free of any mind drama. Now she was in the Queen energy which was full of power, confidence, and femininity always looking out for the greater good of others.

I'm every girls dream
Classy Royal and Supreme;
I flaunt all my loveliness in
Luxurious Sheen
I'm a Queen
I'm a Queen
I'm a Queen
Pride is my asset
And Honour is all mine,
I exist where power and splendour have been;
I'm a Queen
I'm a Queen
I'm a Queen
Oh so' I have so many characters to play,
As strong as a Hero
As fair as a Judge
As shrewd as a Serpent and heart full of Love;
To keep up to the faith you have in me
As if I have seen the unseen…
All for the promise I have given to reign,
And serve you forever as a Queen….
I'm a Queen
I'm a Queen
I'm a Queen

CHAPTER 18
AGONY

Real Agony lies in the eyes that saw behind the million smiles

More exposure Mira got, all the more people she met from different walks of life. Meeting new people allowed her to restate what her life looks like and how she can make it better. It also allowed her to reflect upon herself and see how she has improved in certain areas of life. Not only she was enjoying her achievements but also found peace in her struggles, because there were so many more out there who were struggling to achieve what she already had. She could now see and feel the pain people were going through in this world and she could see there was not even a single 'perfect story'.

Everyone has a story and every story is different !!

The eyes that saw beyond a million smiles,
A slithering pain,
The once blooming flowers
Went down the memory lane
Now lay torn and completely frozen;
Waiting for one streak of sunshine, a ray of hope
Where the smiles become real
And the flowers learn to blossom in the coldest zone;
And see where the real agony lies, it is in enduring the eyes that saw beyond a million smiles….

CHAPTER 19
MYSTERIES LIVE AND MYSTERIOUS ARE KNOWN

Mysteries live and mysterious are known

Mira thought 'It is extremely easy to get trapped by the circumstances, expectations or perceptions by which we are valued or respected in society. We all want to have a different direction in our lives, but we are held back by the insatiable desires or fears that are incompatible with that freedom. We succumb to the circumstances, even without our knowledge because we are ruled by the fear of mind. She understood life pretty well, its soul purpose and it's consequences but still at times she would wonder why things don't always happen the way we want. Ultimately we cannot control life and life just happens and that's the biggest mystery.

Everything starts within us and must end within us too. life is a mystery.

Universe has its mysterious call,
Sometimes the desires rise sometimes they fall ;
Numerous questions come to the mind,
Even when you stay on the grind……
Why is Sun's corona so hot ?
Can you find an answer for that, no surely not
Why moon has to borrow someone else's light ?
To lighten the world to its brightest bright
You always give up counting the stars,
While as a child it seemed easiest by far ;
Why a cool soothing breeze suddenly wears a mask ?
Of a roaring wild wind which has a deadly task ;
How birds take their beautiful flight
and come down to rest in the night.
How can there be countless species living on the planet earth,
Later left as cremains, which describes their worth ;
Our faith is strong in Almighty and we know everything will be fine,
Even when we can only feel the invisible Divine !!
There is still one thing that bothers me all the more,
That humans are more mysterious, isn't it for sure ??
A lifetime feels a way too short to discover their mysteries,
Tied to their foible, quirky, unexplained characteristic theories ;
We are the curious souls
Trying to find answers all unknown,
This explains the way of life
MYSTERIES LIVE AND MYSTERIOUS ARE KNOWN !!!!

CHAPTER 20
DESIRE

True love stories never have endings

The desire to be loved is an illusion, don't get so attached to it that you lose yourself in it'

The desire to be loved is an innate human desire. We all crave connection and affection in some form or another. It's a basic human need like food, water and shelter. So you should not be afraid to let the desire for love and connection guide you. Everyone is worthy of love.

But Mira started thinking differently after being hurt, abused and used in the relationship as pure as marriage. She lost all trust in love and thought that this desire to be loved comes from a fear of loneliness. For the warrior that she had become fearlessness had sinked deep into her. As human beings are created for love, relationships and communities, we all need to be understood. We all long for acceptance. As Mira faced this world and its hardships alone so she never wanted to live in the illusion of love. She wanted something different something rare, a soulful and divine connection. She wanted to believe that true love stories never have endings.

> Be rain to my clouds to roll down the thunder !!

CHAPTER 21
MYSTIC WALK

She is a Mystic Goddess, in synch with her power, ready to change the world

The trials of life had taught Mira to be wise. Her peace of mind had become her most valuable asset that she wouldn't compromise it for anything. She had become more profound and deep in her approach towards life and self, directly apprehended by the experiences she had on that path. The mystical path for her was about surrender. Rather than her mind she followed her feelings. As she started loving herself enough to nourish every level of her being and her true needs, she found an infinite reservoir of life blooming in her and she became so full of life that every where she went she would only spread positivity and happiness. She discovered that happiness is an inner thing. Someone or the other will try to make you miserable but it's your choice to be shallow and unhappy or to be wise and happy. A mystic's journey is into the heart of existence itself and one can only experience it by diving deep into it.

> She lives in her own world
> Discovering the known yet unknown
> Mystery to all and discovery to none,
> It's her mystic walk
> Where she lets her soul talk;
> Shrouded in deep secrecy
> Fathoming her own prophecy
> It's her mystic walk
> Where she lets her soul talk ;
> Blooming inch by inch in sheer joy,
> Trying from within to let it uncoy
> To let in uncoy
> It's her mystic walk
> Where she lets her soul talk…….

Read Below to win interesting cash prizes

They say life is a puzzle which is best left unsolved. Same way the author has left an unsolved mystery in the narrative poetry book. She left it incomplete and complete in a way.

So are you curious to know whether Mira is still alive or dead. Is she divorced or is she still in the same relationship? If you are curious to find answers to all these questions then let's make it more interesting and exciting. Let's give out some convincing answers to this seemingly unanswered story of Mira. On the next page you will find a series of questions and a scan code. This QR Code will lead you to the page where you can fill in your answers based on what you think would have happened in Mira's story and that's where you find the truth about Mira's life. There are exciting cash prizes worth rupees 11000 and 5000 on bringing structure to Mira's story and answering the questions correctly. So what are you waiting for ? The contest is open until the final date of submission on google form. Don't miss the opportunity. Scan the QR Code, enter the contest and win cash prizes.

ABOUT THE AUTHOR

Shivali Kalra, has a lot of titles to her credit, A fashion designer, an entrepreneur, a writer, a Social Activist and above all an Emotional & Mental Health Professional. She has learnt to pave the way to success by mere transforming the challenges into opportunities in all her endeavours. She has always stood in the face of adversities by defying her limitations that helped her gain intensive knowledge by mastering her skills and acquiring expertise in whatever she does. Writing has always been author's hobby and passion. Her writings are the reflection of her inner wisdom. After few years of writing poems, quotations and short stories, she decided to publish few of her poems crafted in her unique style in the form of a story. She calls them Narrative Poetry. Her work and achievements across these multiple areas broadly addresses the narrative of human experience. In her simple writings she loves to unlock the key emotions as well as imagery and structural thoughts behind the most complexed narrative.

But she says the best title to her credit is that of mother besides all other titles that she holds in her professional and personal life.

www.ingramcontent.com/pod-product-compliance
Lightning Source LLC
LaVergne TN
LVHW041540070526
838199LV00046B/1759